Get Motoring!
Airplanes

by Dalton Rains

FOCUS READERS.
SCOUT

www.focusreaders.com

Copyright © 2024 by Focus Readers®, Mendota Heights, MN 55120. All rights reserved. No part of this book may be reproduced or utilized in any form or by any means without written permission from the publisher.

Focus Readers is distributed by North Star Editions: sales@northstareditions.com | 888-417-0195

Produced for Focus Readers by Red Line Editorial.

Photographs ©: Shutterstock Images, cover, 1, 4, 7 (top), 7 (bottom), 8–9, 11, 13, 15, 16 (top left), 16 (top right), 16 (bottom left), 16 (bottom right)

Library of Congress Cataloging-in-Publication Data
Names: Rains, Dalton, author.
Title: Airplanes / Dalton Rains.
Description: Mendota Heights, MN : Focus Readers, [2024] | Series: Get motoring! | Includes index. | Audience: Grades K-1
Identifiers: LCCN 2023026642 (print) | LCCN 2023026643 (ebook) | ISBN 9798889980056 (hardcover) | ISBN 9798889980483 (paperback) | ISBN 9798889981336 (ebook pdf) | ISBN 9798889980919 (hosted ebook)
Subjects: LCSH: Airplanes--Juvenile literature.
Classification: LCC TL547 .R325 2024 (print) | LCC TL547 (ebook) | DDC 629.133/34--dc23/eng/20230725
LC record available at https://lccn.loc.gov/2023026642
LC ebook record available at https://lccn.loc.gov/2023026643

Printed in the United States of America
Mankato, MN
012024

About the Author

Dalton Rains is a writer and editor who lives in Minnesota.

Table of Contents

Airplanes 5

Parts 8

Inside 12

Glossary 16

Index 16

Airplanes

Airplanes fly in the sky.

They can move very fast.

Some airplanes are large.

Others are small.

Airplanes fly out of airports.

airport

7

Parts

Airplanes have **engines**. Some engines are under the wings.

Airplanes also have **wheels**.

Wheels help airplanes take off.

Wheels also help airplanes land.

Inside

Airplanes have **seats** inside.

People sit in them.

There are many rows of seats.

Airplanes help people travel. People can look out the **windows** while they fly.

Glossary

engines

wheels

seats

windows

Index

A
airports, 6

L
land, 10

T
travel, 14

W
wings, 8